# Iowa

Jill Wheeler

Visit us at
www.abdopublishing.com

Published by ABDO Publishing Company, 8000 West 78th Street, Suite 310, Edina, Minnesota 55439 USA. Copyright ©2010 by Abdo Consulting Group, Inc. International copyrights reserved in all countries. No part of this book may be reproduced in any form without written permission from the publisher. The Checkerboard Library™ is a trademark and logo of ABDO Publishing Company.

Printed in the United States.

**Editor:** John Hamilton
**Graphic Design:** Sue Hamilton
**Cover Illustration:** Neil Klinepier
**Cover Photo:** iStock Photo

Manufactured with paper containing at least 10% post-consumer waste

**Interior Photo Credits:** AP Images, Corbis, iStock Photo, Melissa Ritter, North Wind Picture Archives, Library of Congress, Heinz Company, Iowa Tourism Office, Secretary of State of Iowa, and the U.S. Geological Survey.
**Statistics:** State population statistics taken from 2008 U.S. Census Bureau estimates. City and town population statistics taken from July 1, 2007, U.S. Census Bureau estimates. Land and water area statistics taken from 2000 Census, U.S. Census Bureau.

Library of Congress Cataloging-in-Publication Data

Wheeler, Jill C., 1964-
  Iowa / Jill C. Wheeler.
      p. cm. -- (The United States)
  Includes index.
  ISBN 978-1-60453-650-8
  1. Iowa--Juvenile literature. I. Title.

F621.3.W48 2010
977.7--dc22
                              2008051040

# Table of Contents

# The Hawkeye State

Iowa is located in the middle of the United States. The 29th state to join the Union, it was part of the Louisiana Purchase. It is known as the Hawkeye State. The name comes from Chief Blackhawk, a Sauk Native American.

Many people think of farming when they think of Iowa. That is no surprise. Iowa farmers grow 18 percent of all the corn produced in the United States. Most of that corn is used to feed cattle and pigs. Those animals are processed and end up in grocery stores as hamburger, steaks, and pork chops.

Iowa is a land of wide-open spaces dotted with farms and small towns. Besides farming, Iowa is known for its excellent public schools, as well as many fine colleges and universities.

A rainbow appears
over an Iowa farm.

# Quick Facts

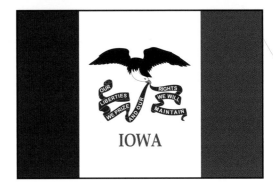

IOWA

**Name:** Iowa comes from the Ioway (a Native American tribe) language and means "this is the place" or "the beautiful land."

**State Capital:** Des Moines
**Date of Statehood:** December 28, 1846 (29th state)
**Population:** 3,002,555 (30th-most populous state)

**Area (Total Land and Water):** 56,272 square miles (145,744 sq km), 26th-largest state

**Largest City:** Des Moines, population 196,998

**Nickname:** The Hawkeye State

**Motto:** Our Liberties We Prize and Our Rights We Will Maintain

**State Bird:** Eastern Goldfinch, also called the Wild Canary

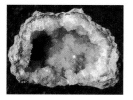

Herbert Hoover

**State Flower:** Wild Rose

**State Rock:** Geode

**State Tree:** Oak

**State Song:** "Song of Iowa"

**Highest Point:** 1,670 feet (509 m), in Osceola County

**Lowest Point:** 480 feet (146 m), in Lee County

**Average July Temperature:** 75°F (24°C)

**Record High Temperature:** 118°F (48°C), July 20, 1934, in Keokuk

**Average January Temperature:** 19°F (-7°C)

**Record Low Temperature:** -47°F (-44°C), January 12, 1912, in Washta

**Average Annual Precipitation:** 34 inches (86 cm)

**Number of U.S. Senators:** 2

**Number of U.S. Representatives:** 5

**U.S. Presidents Born in Iowa:** Herbert Hoover (1874-1964), 31st president

**U.S. Postal Service Abbreviation:** IA

# Geography

Iowa's geography is perfect for farming. Four giant sheets of ice called glaciers covered most of the land about two million years ago. Because of these glaciers, Iowa's land is very flat. The land is covered with rich soil called till.

The glaciers also created many rivers. Most of the rivers in Iowa are small. The small rivers flow into two large rivers, the Mississippi and the Missouri. The Missouri River runs along most of the west side of Iowa. The Big Sioux River runs along the northwest corner of the state. The Mississippi River flows along the east side of Iowa. This makes Iowa the only state whose east and west borders are rivers.

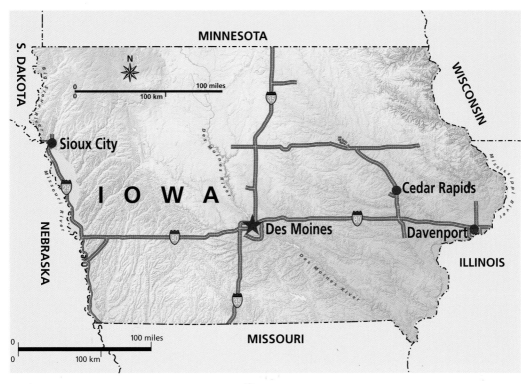

Iowa's total land and water area is 56,272 square miles (145,744 sq km). It is the 26th-largest state. The state capital is Des Moines.

When the glaciers melted, they left behind soil. The Loess Hills in western Iowa were formed by this soil. These hills are covered in hardwood forests and prairie grass. Many animals make their home in the Loess Hills. These animals include bobcats, badgers, gray foxes,

The Loess Hills in western Iowa.

pheasants, and red-tailed hawks. The Loess Hills are a favorite place for students and families to visit.

A red-tailed hawk sits on a fence post.

Iowa is the nation's 26th-largest state by size. It is 56,272 square miles (145,744 sq km), mostly plains. Iowa is the largest producer of corn and soybeans in the United States.

Most of Iowa is farmland. There is more farmland in Iowa than any other type of land. Iowa has about 93,000 farms, totaling 30.7 million acres (12.4 million ha) of farmland. There are less than two million acres (809,371 ha) of forest in Iowa. That means Iowa has about 17 times as much farmland as forest. Much of the rest of Iowa is made up of sloping hills, limestone bluffs, and forests.

Most of Iowa is farmland.

A limestone cave in Iowa.

# Climate and Weather

Iowa's summers are very hot and humid. This climate provides good growing conditions for soybeans, corn, and other crops. The average growing season is 140 days in the north and 170 days in the south.

Iowa's winters are harsh. There are strong winds and lots of snow. There is usually snow on the ground from December until March.

The temperature can change up to 50 degrees Fahrenheit (10°C) in one day. Air pressure changes often bring thunderstorms. Iowa is part of Tornado Alley.

Iowa is very flat. Trees are often used as windbreaks, which help keep soil from blowing away. Iowa gets about 34 inches (86 cm) of rain and snow each year. When rain arrives quickly, flooding can happen.

A tornado strikes Ames, Iowa.

# Plants and Animals

Before settlers came, 80 percent of Iowa was covered with prairie grass. Today, 88 percent of Iowa is farmland, and about 5 percent is woodland.

There are 12 different kinds of oak trees native to Iowa. Other common trees are hickory, maple, elm, walnut, cherry, willow, and cottonwood.

The four major state forests are the Shimek, Stephens, Yellow River, and Loess Hills.

Some of the most common wildflowers in Iowa include pasqueflowers, asters, phlox, lilies, and wild indigo brooms. Iowa also has several special flower centers and celebrations. Dutch immigrants settled the city of Pella and brought tulips with them. Today, the Pella Tulip Time Festival is held each year in May.

A windmill stands in the town of Pella, Iowa, home of the Pella Tulip Time Festival.

The Bellevue State Park butterfly garden attracts more than 60 kinds of butterflies. These butterflies are important in flower pollination.

A curious raccoon.

Iowa is also home to many different types of animals, including foxes, white-tailed deer, muskrats, raccoons, coyotes, mink, skunks, groundhogs, rabbits, badgers, and weasels. The state has poisonous snakes, too, like the prairie, massasauga, and timber rattlesnakes.

Iowa is an excellent place to watch bird migrations. Some birds travel all the way from the Arctic to the Gulf of Mexico. Roughly half a million snow geese pass through Iowa each year. Iowa is also a prime bird hunting area. The state is famous for ring-necked pheasant hunting. Partridges, turkeys, and quail are also hunted.

Ring-Necked Pheasant

Snow Goose

Turkey

# History

When the glaciers that once covered Iowa melted, they left behind flat, rich soil. The first Native Americans to arrive were the Paleo-Indians. They were hunters.

Several hundred years later, the Woodland people (or

Ma-Has-Kah, or White Cloud, an Ioway chief.

Mound Builders) lived in Iowa. They grew squash and corn. To honor their dead, they built huge mounds of dirt shaped like bears and birds.

Other Native American tribes in Iowa included the Ioway, Sauk, Mesaquakie, Oto, Illinois, Miami, Sioux, and Missouri.

Jacques Marquette and Louis Joliet traveled and explored along the Mississippi River in 1673.

The first European explorers came to Iowa in 1673. Jacques Marquette and Louis Joliet explored around the Mississippi River. René-Robert Cavelier de La Salle explored the area in 1682. He claimed the land for France.

Iowa was not a part of the United States until 1803. President Thomas Jefferson bought 800,000 square miles (2 million sq km) of land from France for $15 million. This land deal was called the Louisiana Purchase. The purchase included Iowa.

In the early 1800s, settlers arrived and started farms. This forced many Native Americans from their homes. Fighting sometimes broke out.

Iowa was originally part of Missouri Territory. In 1838, it became a separate territory called Iowa Territory. In 1846, Iowa became the 29th state. The first governor was Ansel Briggs.

Ansel Briggs

The American Civil War began in 1861 and divided the states over the issue of slavery. Iowa was against slavery. Iowa leaders sent 75,000 troops to fight for the North.

World War I started in 1914. During the war, Iowa sold crops to European countries. The demand for food was high. Farmers borrowed money to buy more land and equipment. Then, World War I ended in 1918. Many farmers could not afford to repay their loans. Some lost their land.

Iowans fought against slavery during the American Civil War. The First Iowa Regiment fought at Wilson's Creek, Missouri, on August 10, 1861.

Things became worse during the Great Depression in the 1930s. Many farms, railroads, and banks lost money. Many people lost their jobs.

The United States entered World War II in 1941. More than 286,000 people from Iowa fought in the war. Pilots were trained in Ottumwa and Iowa City. Bombs and bullets were made in Ankeny and Burlington.

The war led to the invention of a lot of machinery. Some of the machines were used on farms. They did work that many people used to do. As a result, more people moved to cities than ever before.

During the Great Flood of 1993, the Missouri, Mississippi, Des Moines, Cedar, and Iowa Rivers overflowed in the spring. Fields were submerged. Even cattle were stranded in the water. Years after the disaster, many areas were still damaged.

The Great Flood of 1993 left much of Iowa underwater, including fields, homes, roads, and businesses.

# Did You Know?

- Iowa and Missouri officials got into a fight in 1839 over the location of the border between the states. Both wanted a small piece of land with three honey trees on it. This war was called the Honey War.

- *Ripley's Believe It Or Not* calls Snake Alley the most crooked street in the world. It is located in Burlington, Iowa. Many people visit this street to walk, bike, or simply look at the strange sight.

Snake Alley in Burlington, Iowa.

- Strawberry Point, Iowa, has the world's largest strawberry statue. It stands next to the town's city hall. The big, red berry is an amazing 15-feet (5-m) tall!

- In the mid 1800s, many Iowans risked their lives to help slaves escape to freedom. They used their homes in the Underground Railroad. The Underground Railroad wasn't a railroad at all. It was a secret network of paths and helpers who led people to freedom.

# People

Author **Laura Ingalls Wilder** (1867-1957) lived in Iowa for part of her childhood.  She wrote about her pioneer experiences in her Little House book series.  There is now a Laura Ingalls Wilder Park and Museum in Burr Oak, Iowa.

**Herbert Hoover** (1874-1964) was born in Iowa and became the 31st president in 1929.  He was president during the start of the Great Depression.  He worked hard to help the nation.  Yet many people thought he was responsible for the problems.  The Herbert Hoover Presidential Library and Museum is in West Branch, Iowa.

**Bob Feller** (1918- ) was a pitcher for the Cleveland Indians baseball team for 20 years. He pitched three no-hitters during his career. He was inducted into the Baseball Hall of Fame in 1962. There is a museum in Feller's honor in his hometown of Van Meter, Iowa.

Bob Feller was called the "Heater from Van Meter."

Iowa farmer **Jesse Hiatt** (1826?-1898) is the father of the Red Delicious apple. In the 1870s, he noticed a wild apple tree growing out of place in his orchard. He cut it down twice, but the tree kept growing back, so he kept it. In the 1880s, he tried the tree's first apples. The fruit was better than any he had ever tasted. He entered the apple in a contest and it won. It was purchased and named the Delicious apple. It became the best-selling apple in the United States.

John Wayne starred in many Western movies, such as *True Grit* and *Rio Lobo*.

Movie star **John Wayne** (1907-1979) was born in Winterset, Iowa. He was born Marion Morisson, but changed his name when he moved to Hollywood. Wayne starred in many Western movies, including *True Grit*, *Rio Lobo*, and *Stagecoach*. His childhood home has been turned into a museum.

**Johnny Carson** (1925-2005) was a famous television host. He was born in Corning, Iowa, in 1925. He hosted *The Tonight Show Starring Johnny Carson* for 30 years. He interviewed many actors, singers, and comedians.

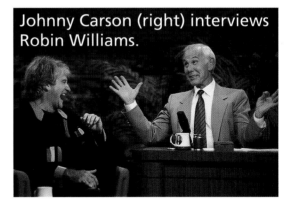

Johnny Carson (right) interviews Robin Williams.

**Esther Pauline Friedman Lederer** (1918-2002) and her sister, **Pauline Esther Friedman Phillips** (1918- ), were famous Iowa twins. Both women wrote advice columns.

"Dear Abby" (left) and her twin sister "Ann Landers."

Esther wrote as Ann Landers. Her sister, Pauline, wrote the column "Dear Abby." Their columns contained letters from readers. The letters were about problems readers were having. The problems were often about love, friends, or family. Esther and Pauline answered their readers' questions. Their columns were carried in newspapers around the world.

# Cities

**Des Moines** is the capital of Iowa.  It is in the center of the state, where the Raccoon and Des Moines Rivers meet.  There are 196,998 people

living in the city.  The people of Des Moines are proud of the city's schools, its arts and culture, and friendly neighborhoods.  Major tourist attractions include the capitol building, the Iowa State Fair, and many memorials.  These memorials include a Civil War memorial, a Spanish-American War memorial, a memorial for the Korean War, and a Vietnam War memorial.

Iowa's second-largest city is **Cedar Rapids**. It is home to 126,396 people. It is considered the manufacturing and art center of Iowa. It is home to the Cedar Rapids Symphony, as well as the Cedar Rapids Museum of Art. There is also a large nature preserve in Cedar Rapids called the Indian Creek Nature Center. The nature center has 210 acres (85 ha) and holds an annual maple syrup festival.

The Cedar Rapids Museum of Art.

**Davenport**, the third-largest city in Iowa, has a population of 98,975 people. It is very close to the Mississippi River. Davenport began as a Native American trading post. It is across the river from Illinois. Davenport and its three neighboring towns are considered the largest metropolitan area between Minneapolis, Minnesota, and St. Louis, Missouri. Channel Cat Water Taxis are open-air boats that travel on the Mississippi to stops in Iowa and Illinois. They provide entertainment for residents and visitors to Davenport.

Davenport is the third-largest city in Iowa. It rests on the shore of the Mississippi River.

**Sioux City** was settled in 1849 but not named until 1854. It is located where the Big Sioux, Floyd, and Missouri Rivers meet. There are 82,684 people who live in Sioux City. It is home to a 30-foot (9-m) -tall stainless steel statue of the Immaculate Heart of Mary, Queen of Peace. Sioux City is also home to the Mid-America Air Museum. This museum has exhibits on the history of flight. The Sergeant Floyd Monument overlooks the Missouri River. Floyd died in 1804 as a member of the Lewis and Clark Expedition. He died of a ruptured appendix.

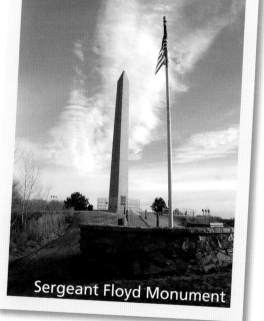
Sergeant Floyd Monument

# Transportation

The first railways in Iowa were built in the 1850s. The first railroad to span the Mississippi River was built in Davenport in 1856. By 1867, a railroad stretched all the way across Iowa to Council Bluffs. Building railroads had both good and bad results.

The railroads increased the state's income because food sold for higher prices in Chicago, Illinois. However, the railroads were expensive.

The Boone & Scenic Valley Railroad still runs out of Boone, Iowa.

Roads began replacing railroads in 1917. The first major road in Iowa was Highway 6, also known as the Great White Way.

The busiest highway in Iowa today is the east-west highway called Interstate 80. About 10,000 cars and trucks pass over this road every day.

Trucks are the most popular method of shipping today.

Trucks are the most popular method of shipping today. Trucks are important to Iowa's commerce. Airplanes are also important. There are eight major airports in Iowa.

# Natural Resources

When you think of Iowa, the first thing that comes to mind may be farming. Iowa helps feed the nation. Almost one-fifth of all the nation's corn is grown in Iowa.

Iowa farmland is very fertile. Two special kinds of rich soil cover Iowa. They are called till and drift. These soils were spread across much of Iowa by glaciers.

Iowa grows almost one-fifth of all the nation's corn.

Iowa's primary crops are corn and soybeans. Farmers also raise hogs and beef cattle. The people of Iowa know how important it is to keep the land fertile. Farmers rotate crops and work to preserve the land.

Iowa has one farm for every 32 people. However, the number of family farms has been steadily decreasing. It takes a lot of money to buy or rent land and run a farm. Even though farming is a difficult life, thousands of people do it every year.

Workers in Iowa mine limestone, sand, and gravel. Iowa is also a leader in dairy production, making butter, cream, and other milk products.

A dairy cow.

# Industry

Heinz has a factory in Muscatine, Iowa.

Farming is very important in Iowa. Yet Iowa also has other important industries.  There are 49,000 jobs in the food processing industry.  Iowa also manufactures chemicals, electrical equipment, machinery, printed materials, plastic products, rubber, ketchup, pudding, medicines, recreational vehicles, and pet food.

Big retail categories in Iowa include automobile sales, grocery stores, and restaurants.  After farm equipment, the biggest sales come from insurance, banking, and real estate.  Gambling is also a big source of state revenue.

There are also quite a few large companies in Iowa. Many software companies make their home in Des Moines. Other companies have operations in Iowa, including Wells Fargo, Heinz, John Deere, and Quaker Oats.

Only eight percent of Iowans are farmers. About 50 percent are teachers, bankers, doctors and nurses, and retail workers. Service industries include health care, banking, finance, and tourism. Tourism is growing in Iowa.

The bridges of Madison County are a popular tourist destination.

# Sports

Iowa does not have any major professional sports teams. Instead, college sports are a big attraction. There are many Iowa universities and colleges that have athletic programs. Iowa City's University of Iowa has sports teams called the Hawkeyes. Football and basketball are their most popular sports.

The teams from Iowa State University, in Ames, are called the Cyclones.

Two famous sports personalities came from Iowa. Glenn "Pop" Warner was a football coach. He invented the double wingback offense.

Dan Gable was a wrestling legend.

Dan Gable of Waterloo is a wrestling legend. In his senior year of high school, he won all 64 of his matches. At Iowa State University, his record was 116-1. He won the gold medal in the 1972 Munich Olympics.

Iowa has many choices for recreation. These include fishing, hunting, horseback riding, skydiving, skiing, soccer, biking, hang gliding, horseshoe pitching, and canoeing. The Wabash Trace Nature Trail is popular with bikers. Iowa also has more than 400 golf courses.

# Entertainment

An interesting Iowa destination is the Grotto of the Redemption in West Bend. This is a huge structure made of rocks, gems, and glass. A priest began building this shrine

Many people visit the Grotto of the Redemption each year.

in 1912. More than 100,000 people visit it each year. Tourists also visit Living History Farms in Urbandale. This museum shows how farms worked throughout Iowa's history. Workers at historic Fort Madison wear costumes from the 1800s. At the Effigy Mounds National Monument in northeastern Iowa, visitors explore animal-shaped mounds made by the Woodland people.

The Desoto National Wildlife Refuge provides a natural habitat for many native animals.

People visit the Amana Colonies to see another culture. In these colonies, people share the work and the land.

Iowa universities offer perfect places for

Visitors learn about Iowa farms at Living History Farms.

symphonies, dances, and musical shows. Many Iowa cities also hold annual fairs. The biggest of these is the Iowa State Fair in Des Moines. There are also at least 9 major art museums, 65 theater groups, 40 musical groups, and 18 music and dance groups in the state.

# Timeline

**1673**—Father Jacques Marquette and Louis Joliet arrive in Iowa via the Mississippi River.

**1682**—All land bordering the Mississippi River (including Iowa) is claimed for France by explorer René-Robert Cavelier de La Salle.

**1788**—Lead is mined by Julien Dubuque in Iowa.

**1803**—The United States gets the Louisiana Purchase, which includes Iowa, from France.

**1838**—Iowa Territory is established. It includes parts of what are now Iowa, North Dakota, South Dakota, and Minnesota.

**1846**—Iowa becomes the 29th state.

**1929-1939**—Many farms are lost due to the Great Depression.

**1993**—Massive flooding causes billions of dollars of damage. This horrible disaster becomes known as the Great Flood of 1993.

**2008**—Barack Obama wins the Iowa Democratic Caucus, the first step on his way to becoming president.

# Glossary

**Appendix**—A body part. It is a small, closed tube leading from the large intestine.

**Drift**—A type of soil.

**Glacier**—A huge, slow-moving sheet of ice that grows and shrinks as the climate changes. The ice sheets can be more than one mile (1.6 km) thick.

**Great Depression**—A time in American history beginning in 1929 and lasting for several years when many businesses failed and millions of people lost their jobs.

**Lewis and Clark Expedition**—An exploration of the west, led by Meriwether Lewis and William Clark, from 1804-1806.

**Limestone**—A hard rock used in buildings and in making lime and cement. Limestone is formed from the remains of shells or coral.

**Louisiana Purchase**—The purchase by the United States of about 530 million acres (214 million ha) of land from France in 1803.

**Migration**—The seasonal movement by birds from a cold climate to a warmer one.

**Plain**—A large, flat area of land.

**Pollination**—The act of transferring pollen from one part of a plant to another part of the same or another plant so that the plant can produce seed.

**Rotate**—To move crops to different areas of land in order to keep the soil fertile and productive.

**Till**—A type of soil.

**Tornado Alley**—An area of the United States that has many tornadoes. Tornado Alley stretches from Texas in the south to North Dakota in the north and east to parts of Ohio.

**Underground Railroad**—A network of people who helped slaves escape to freedom.

# Index